*W*HEN YOUR FAMILY IS LIVING
WITH MENTAL ILLNESS

DIFFICULT TIMES SERIES

WHEN YOUR FAMILY IS LIVING WITH MENTAL ILLNESS

MARCIA LUND

Augsburg Books · MINNEAPOLIS

*To my brother Dave for helping me
open the door to an new understanding
of mental illness.*

WHEN YOUR FAMILY IS LIVING WITH MENTAL ILLNESS

Large-quantity purchases or custom editions of this book are available at a discount from the publisher. For more information, contact the sales department at Augsburg Fortress, Publishers, 1-800-328-4648, or write to: Sales Director, Augsburg Fortress, Publishers, P.O. Box 1209, Minneapolis, MN 55440-1209.

Cover design by David Meyer
Book design by Jessica A. Klein

Library of Congress Cataloging-in-Publication Data
Lund, Marcia, 1959-
  When your family is living with mental illness / by Marcia Lund.
    p. cm.
  Includes bibliographical references.
  ISBN   978-0-8066-4423-3
    1. Mentally ill—Family relationships—Popular works. I. Title.
RC455.4.F3 L86 2002
616.89—dc21   2002074573

The paper used in this publication meets the minimum requirements of American National Standard for Information Sciences—Permanence of Paper for Printed Library Materials, ANSI Z329.48-1984. ♾ ™

Manufactured in the U.S.A.

—ᴍ— *Contents* —ᴍ—

126761

—⚹—

"*I am fortunate that I have not died from my illness, fortunate in having received the best medical care available, and fortunate in having the friends, colleagues, and the family I do. . . . I am tired of hiding, tired of misspent and knotted energies, tired of the hypocrisy, and tired of acting as though I have something to hide. . . . I continue to have concerns about my decision to be public about my illness, but one of the advantages of having had manic-depressive illness for more than thirty years is that very little seems insurmountably difficult.*"

—Kay Redfield Jamison,
An Unquiet Mind
(New York: Knopf, 1995)
Used by permission.

—⚹—

—∞— *A Word to the Reader* —∞—

The pain of knowing a family member has a mental illness seems insurmountable at first—the initial shock and grief of the news, the need to make choices about medical professionals, treatment, safety, and finances add to the burden. But there is hope.

Much of this book presents the information I have found helpful as a sister of a man with schizophrenia. For many years I dealt with the pain of my brother's illness by burying it, keeping it hidden from myself and others. I was afraid to face the illness, afraid to learn about it, afraid to be in my brother's presence, and afraid to talk with others.

Then, in my late thirties, *I* became mentally ill, slumping into a deep depression due to a number of life changes and overwork. Whether or not I realized it at the time, I retreated into isolation, trapped in pain, unable to work or live in the ways I had always known before. Ironically, it was the experience with my brother that gave me some of the tools and willingness to take action on my own behalf. I knew I had to call a therapist, I knew I would have to treat the depression with medication, I knew I had to change my work situation and overall lifestyle, I knew that I had to rely on family and friends to help pull me out of the frozen state of entrapment I felt, and I knew I had to start to pray for healing and wholeness.

When I reached my darkest and most vulnerable state, I realized there was no point in hiding my illness.

In order to move forward and grow, I needed to share my experience with others and listen to others describe how they found relief, new purpose, and hope. When I discovered I was not alone, the floodgates opened. Sharing my pain allowed me to let go of its hold on me. Of course, this didn't cure my depression or cure my brother's illness, but it became possible to view mental illness in a different light.

The chapters in this book reveal some of the essential ways family members can deal with mental illness. Chapter 1 underscores the value of knowing you are not alone or solely responsible for the person with mental illness. Chapter 2 helps family members identify the symptoms of mental illness. Chapter 3 gives information on choosing doctors or methods of treatment. Chapter 4 addresses some of the ways family members can reach out to a brother or sister, parent or child with mental illness, as well as find resources to stay informed and healthy themselves. Chapter 5 takes a look at the idea of living in hope. Each day brings new challenges for persons with mental illness and their families. Hope lies in the belief that if we face the challenges and make the right choices, healing and recovery will happen one day at a time.

To families of persons with mental illness, I offer what I have found helpful: Be kind to them, show them they are valued and cherished, learn about their illness, stay informed, remember to keep the right attitude, ask them what they want in life, and find ways to accept the pain you are dealing with by sharing your stories with others.

—m— *Chapter One* —m—
You Are Not Alone

Rain Man

Most of us who have tried to deal with mental illness in our family without seeking help know how frustrating and counterproductive it can be. A classic example of this kind of frustration is portrayed in the movie *Rain Man*. Charlie Babbit, one of the main characters in the movie, learns that his estranged father has died. In his father's will, Charlie receives his father's rose bushes and his antique car. The rest of his father's estate ($3 million) is willed to another person. Charlie is infuriated and determined to find out who the person is. After some hunting, Charlie discovers that the $3 million has been put in a trust fund for his brother, Raymond. Charlie's initial reaction is shock. He isn't even aware that he has a brother. Raymond's guardian reveals to Charlie that his brother was sent to an institution when Charlie was very young.

Feeling cheated out of the estate money, Charlie tries to convince his brother's guardian to split the money awarded to Raymond, but the guardian refuses to make a deal. In desperation, Charlie decides to kidnap his brother and hold him in custody until he can make a deal to get a portion of the money.

During the few days they are together, Charlie finds out a number of things about Raymond. He

begins to learn how Raymond processes information, lives according to a rigid routine, and needs
constant supervision. When Charlie arranges a flight
from Cincinnati to Los Angeles (where Charlie
lives), Raymond throws his first major tantrum,
protesting that flying is not safe and listing the exact
statistics of plane crashes for each airline. So Charlie
decides to drive with Raymond to L.A. In various
hotels en route to L.A., Raymond has to comfort
himself with something familiar before he can
adjust to the new surroundings. Most of the time he
uses the Abbott and Costello monologue "Who's on
first?" each time he enters a new hotel room. In addition, Raymond needs to keep his routine of eating at
the same time each day and watching his favorite
television programs to sustain his comfort. Charlie
also discovers that he cannot leave Raymond alone
or unattended, even for a few minutes. During a rest
stop, Charlie asks Raymond to sit in the car for a
short time so he can make a phone call, but when he
returns to the car, Raymond is gone. Charlie finds
him wandering around in the middle of a street
holding up traffic.

Charlie realizes by the end of their trip that no
matter how much he loves his brother, no matter
how much money he can provide, Raymond is in a
world of his own. And without the proper care, there
is a chance that Raymond could harm himself or be
harmed because of the way he thinks and processes
information. Charlie knows he cannot possibly
spend twenty-four hours a day with Raymond,

watching him, protecting him, and caring for him. In the end, Charlie gives up and surrenders his control, allowing Raymond's guardian to take over. But Charlie doesn't lose everything when he makes this decision. He gains a new understanding of what it means to love someone with a mental illness.

Gaining a Brother

Watching *Rain Man* has helped me cope with my own frustrations of having a brother with a mental illness. When I was thirteen and my brother was seventeen, he started to change dramatically. He started to isolate himself more and behave differently. At that time, I didn't really know what was happening. I was afraid of the unpredictability of his behavior. He would become angry about something trivial and punch his fist into the wall or yell at me for no reason at all. I never knew what was going to happen when I was with him, so I gradually withdrew from him as a way of coping.

A year later my brother went to college, so I saw him only during holidays and in the summer. A few years later, he tried to commit suicide. I was living abroad, thousands of miles from home, and could not be there when he was hospitalized and then institutionalized. But I was aware of the impact his illness had on my family. He had been diagnosed with paranoid schizophrenia. For years I dealt with his illness by detaching myself from him, afraid that the same thing might happen to me and unsure how I could interact with him.

Ironically, it was my own struggle with depression about sixteen years later that woke me up! I was thirty-five years old, a mother, a full-time teacher, a tennis instructor, and an editor for a publishing company. Suddenly, I was experiencing the numbing effects of mental illness under my own skin. A series of minor episodes of depression culminated into a major bout of depression triggered by overwork and burnout. In spite of all my determination to continue working, I couldn't find the strength to get out of bed in the morning.

I started talking with others who had struggled with depression. They confirmed the fact that mental illness is common and that recovery is possible. Using a combination of strategies, including medication, psychotherapy, a drastic change in my work situation, and more attention to spirituality and prayer, my health improved over time. Phone calls from friends and family, letters of encouragement, exercise, sharing meals with others, spending less time alone, and taking time to do the things I really enjoyed also made the difference.

As a result of my own experience, I developed more of a respect for my brother and the challenges of having a mental illness. I started calling him on a regular basis, writing letters, bringing him groceries when he ran out of food. The more interaction we had, the more I remembered the days of our childhood and the things we did together. I was beginning to see the brother I knew when I was younger, before he had schizophrenia. We started to connect in new ways. We still have conflicts and difficult times, but our interaction is grounded in a new understanding and acceptance of mental illness. That makes all the difference in the world.

MAKING CONNECTIONS

Currently, my brother lives about five minutes from my apartment. He lives alone, he works part-time, and he continues to be the best sports enthusiast I have ever known.

In my recent encounters with my brother, I have discovered things that help me be more attentive to his illness and recovery. One Sunday I delivered some groceries to his apartment. He invited me in to chat. Immediately, I sensed an auditory overload. He had Handel's *Messiah* playing on his turntable, a football game on the radio, the television was on, and he was listening to music on his headphones. Well, it wasn't the best setup for having a conversation with him. My first inclination was to ask him to turn something off; anything would help. But I didn't. I talked with him while all this music and announcing was going on. That was the day my brother explained that he turned music on to drown out the voices in his own head.

Knowing the reason for all the commotion in his apartment, knowing that it made him comfortable, gave me the motivation to be able to sit with him for twenty minutes listening to the various sounds. The important part was that he was able to talk with me. In fact, the background noise allowed him to be able to carry on a conversation.

Another discovery I have made over the years is that many people who have suffered from trauma to the head or some kind of mental illness retain some part of their talent or expertise from the time before the illness. In my brother's case, he was a terrific athlete before he became ill. He was a lifeguard, played hockey, tennis, basketball, baseball—almost any sport. After he became ill, it was more difficult for him to participate in the sports, but now he continues to stay actively involved by reading the paper and watching sports on television. If on any day I want to know the scores or updates on any team playing a sport, I can call Dave and he will know everything—the scores, the highlights, the names of the players, and their records. Even though he doesn't play tennis anymore, and hasn't for years, if Dave and I go out on a tennis court to hit balls, his technique for hitting ground strokes and serves is so smooth and fluid, it is as if he never put down his racket.

My ability to connect with my brother came about because I became more attentive to what mental illness is and more willing to learn from him. The biggest obstacle had been my own fear, fear that grew out of myths and distorted views of what I thought mental illness was. Once I experienced depression first hand, and other people shared their stories with me, I gained a new understanding and acceptance.

Now, I have the courage to face mental illness, accept it, and befriend it in myself and others. Once I realized that I didn't need to spend so much energy trying to hide my illness or my brother's illness, I put those energies into constructive ways to connect and build stronger bonds with family members, friends, coworkers, children, and others struggling with mental illness.

The toughest ongoing challenge for all persons living with mental illness is making this invisible disease visible so treatment and recovery can begin. How do we do this? First, we need to pay close attention to the family member and learn to recognize the signs of mental illness.

—∞— *Chapter Two* —∞—

Recognizing the Signs of Mental Illness

On January 3, 2001, the United States Surgeon General, David Satcher, M.D., reported that "one in ten children and adolescents suffer from mental illness severe enough to cause some level of impairment. Estimates report only one in five of these children receives treatment." At the adult level, the number of persons who seek help is about the same, one in five.

A number of factors prevent individuals from seeking treatment for mental illnesses, but for those who do ask for help, the success rate for recovery is high. The treatment success rate for a first episode of schizophrenia is 60 percent, 65 to 70 percent for major depression, and 80 percent for bipolar illness.[1]

The most critical part about identifying mental illness is early detection. The sooner the individual begins to receive help and treatment, the more likely the person will learn strategies to recover from the illness. What is so baffling about identifying mental illnesses is the fact that the person with the mental illness may not know what is happening. Therefore, it is necessary for others to help him or her define what the illness is. Furthermore, depending on the age of the person with the illness, there may be an inclination to hide or deny the illness, or worse, cover it up by taking illegal drugs, drinking, or engaging in other destructive behaviors as a way to self medicate. Left untreated, mental illness can be devastating—resulting in a serious accident, suicide attempt, or death.

Family members are, in most cases, the first to recognize a change in an individual's behavior, mood, or personality. They see the person on a daily basis, have a long history together, and have some perspective. They can initiate an evaluation or assessment, but it takes a trained professional to make a thorough assessment and initiate ongoing patient visits to pay close attention to the treatment program and recovery. Family members provide the bridge to recovery—they assist the person by recognizing the signs of mental illness first.

What is mental illness?

The AMI—Wisconsin Family and Consumer Guide defines mental illness as "a group of brain disorders that cause severe disturbances in thinking, feeling, and relating, often resulting in an inability to cope with the ordinary demands of life."[2] Family members from the Arizona Alliance for the Mentally Ill compiled the following list of warning signs of mental illness: (It is important to remember that the severity or frequency of symptoms may be different for each individual. In most cases, a person with mental illness will experience a number of the thought, mood, and behavioral characteristics in the following list. One symptom, such as the inability to concentrate, does not determine a person is mentally ill. But multiple symptoms and the severity of the symptoms could be an indication of illness. In such cases, an assessment or evaluation by a medical doctor or psychiatrist is recommended.)

SYMPTOMS OF MENTAL ILLNESS

1. Changes in thinking or perceiving
- Hallucinations
- Delusions
- Excessive fears or suspiciousness
- Inability to concentrate

2. Changes in mood
- Sadness coming out of nowhere, unrelated to events or circumstances
- Extreme excitement or euphoria
- Pessimism; perceiving the world as gray and lifeless
- Expressions of hopelessness
- Loss of interest in once pleasurable activities
- Thinking or talking about suicide

3. Changes in behavior
- Sitting and doing nothing
- Friendlessness; abnormal self involvement
- Dropping out of activities; decline in academic or athletic performance
- Hostility from one formerly pleasant and friendly
- Indifference, even in highly important situations
- Inability to express joy
- Inappropriate laughter

- Inability to concentrate or cope with minor problems
- Irrational statements
- Peculiar use of words or language structure
- Excessive fears or suspiciousness
- Involvement in automobile accidents
- Drug or alcohol abuse
- Forgetfulness and loss of valuable possessions
- Attempts to escape through geographic change; frequent moves or trips
- Bizarre behavior (skipping, staring, strange posturing)
- Unusual sensitivity to noises, light, clothing

4. Physical changes
- Hyperactivity or inactivity or alternations of these
- Deterioration in hygiene or personal care
- Unexplained weight gain or loss
- Sleeping too much or being unable to sleep[3]

In addition to the broader range of symptoms, there are specific warning signs related to three major mental illnesses: schizophrenia, depression, and bipolar illness (manic depression). What follows is a brief description of these illnesses and the signs that may indicate a person needs treatment.

Schizophrenia

Schizophrenia is a brain disorder that affects approximately two million Americans.

It is associated with genetic factors, chemical imbalances, environmental factors, and abnormalities in brain structure. Schizophrenia affects a person's thinking and judgment, sensory perception, and the ability to interpret and respond to situations or stimuli.[4]

Common symptoms of schizophrenia include: hallucinations (hearing, feeling, or seeing things that exist only in the mind of the individual), delusions (persistent false beliefs), suspiciousness, withdrawal, communication difficulties, and/or drastic changes in behavior and personality.

EARLY WARNING SIGNS FOR SCHIZOPHRENIA

Age Factor
A major psychotic episode (extreme change in ability to function in daily life or activities) may be the first indication of the illness. In men, the disease becomes apparent in the late teens and early twenties. In women, an episode may occur in the late twenties.

Change in Behavior
Watch for drastic changes—inability to sleep or concentrate; withdrawal; drifting away from friends, families, activities; and an increased sense of fear or suspiciousness.

Changes in Appearance
Be aware of signs of poor hygiene or inattentiveness to appearance.

Changes in Thinking

Drastic shifts in thought from paranoia to grandiose delusions (false beliefs) are associated with schizophrenia. Auditory or visual hallucinations (hearing, feeling, or seeing things that exist only in the mind of the individual) are common. Thought processes change radically. Dr. E. Fuller Torrey, one of the leading researchers of schizophrenia, describes the shifts in thinking in this way:

> Think of having a phone operator in the midst of the brain's limbic system, receiving all sensory input, thoughts, ideas, memories and emotions, sorting them, and synthesizing those which go together. In schizophrenia, the switchboard operator is unable to do a good job of sorting and synthesizing, resulting in the impairment of the ability to think logically, feelings of being disconnected, loosening of associations, concreteness and sometimes using neologisms (made-up words).[5]

Changes in Emotions

Watch for radical shifts in emotions, flatness, apathy or inappropriateness in expressing emotion.

DEPRESSION

Depression affects more than nine million adults in the United States. In many respects, depression is an invisible disease. Persons with depression often live their daily lives without noticeable disruption to others. Left untreated, however, the illness may be life threatening.

"Major depression is a biologically based brain disease, not a weakness."[6] All of us have experienced feelings of sadness or being blue, but major depression is a serious medical illness that affects thoughts, behavior, and physical health over a prolonged period of time. Major depression is associated with a prolonged and profound sadness that lasts at least two weeks and causes a significant change in an individual's life.

Major depression is not restricted to a specific age group, race, class, or gender. It affects children, adolescents, adults, and elderly persons. About one in fifteen men will experience the illness, and one in seven women will experience a depression sometime in her lifetime.

"There is not one single cause for major depression."[7] A chemical imbalance in the brain, family history, and genetic factors may contribute to the illness. In addition, difficult life events, such as a death in the family, loss, or chronic stress may trigger an episode, but some persons experience depression separate from a major life crisis.

EARLY WARNING SIGNS FOR DEPRESSION

Changes in Sleep
Difficulty falling asleep, waking up frequently during the night, or waking up an hour to several hours earlier than desired in the morning is common for persons suffering from major depression. Others report they sleep more than usual, often waking up and not feeling rested.

Changes in Appetite
Many persons lose their appetite and lose weight. Others increase the amount of food they eat and gain weight. In many cases, people report food does not appeal to them.

Impaired Concentration and Decision Making
This is an area that causes a tremendous amount of anxiety for a person with the illness.

Reading an article in the newspaper or following the story line in a television show may be difficult. In addition, making choices about what to wear or what product to buy at a grocery store may become difficult.

Loss of Energy
Periods of tremendous fatigue and slowness in thinking processes are common. Responses to external stimuli and generating new ideas is diminished.

Loss of Interest
People experiencing major depression report they lose interest in their usual activities. Things that have given them great pleasure, such as eating and making love, no longer are enjoyable. Other activities may seem unrewarding or boring.

Low Self-Esteem
Thoughts of worthlessness and guilt increase. Persons often dwell on past losses or failures to prove their worthlessness. Negative thoughts, such as, "I am not worth much," pervade the person's thinking.

Feelings of Hopelessness
Strong feelings of hopelessness, of the belief that
nothing will ever improve, can lead to thoughts of
suicide or destructive behavior.

Watch for Alcohol or Drug Abuse
Alcohol is a depressant. If persons suffering from
depression use alcohol to self medicate, the depression may intensify. In addition, alcohol or drug use
could increase levels of anxiety.

Manic-Depression (Bipolar Illness)

Manic-depression is a brain disorder that is charac-
terized by severe mood swings from periods of deep
depression to periods of mania, feelings of euphoria
and highs. Typically, there are normal moods in
between the intense shifts, but some people experience rapid cycles shifting back and forth from
depression to mania without stable periods in
between. More than two million Americans are
affected by bipolar illness each year.

Early Warning Signs for Manic-Depression

Age Factor
Bipolar illness usually becomes apparent during
childhood, adolescence, or early adulthood. It rarely
develops after the age of thirty-five.

Manic Phase
The mania could last for a few days or up to three months in duration, if untreated. Usually the phase is followed by a leveling-off period with normal moods, but in some cases, the depressive phase could follow the manic phase immediately.

Excessive Euphoria
Take note of a family member if he or she reports feeling "on top of the world" and it seems excessive or beyond the normal range of the events in the person's life or typical behavior.

Risky Behavior
Pay attention to comments about not being able to sleep for many nights in a row, a schedule that is unrealistically packed with activities, reckless driving, spending sprees, or other "risky" types of behavior.

Grandiose Delusions
Listen to comments that reflect unwarranted optimism and lack of judgment. Persons with a bipolar illness may have grandiose delusions that lead them to believe they have a special connection with God, celebrities, or political leaders.[8] Hallucinations may be possible.

Flight of Ideas
When a person with bipolar illness talks, it may come out as a rush of ideas. Pay attention to how the

person communicates. If his or her words are a non-stop flight of ideas and the person shifts topics abruptly, this may be sign of the illness.

Distractibility
The person may show patterns of easy distractibility to unimportant details.

Sudden Irritability, Rage, or Paranoia
If the person's grandiose plans or intentions are thwarted, the person may show signs of sudden irritability, rage, or paranoia.

Following the mania phase, a person with manic depression may slip into a depression. The warning signs for this phase follow the path of persons who experience only depression (see previous section).

Persons with mental illness need to be treated as persons first. They have dreams and wishes just like all of us. Woven into their personalities and thoughts is a biological brain disorder that is treatable. There should be no shame or guilt or fear attached to having a mental illness. Family members and friends play a major role in guiding their brothers, sisters, children, friends, or parents to a kind of life that is satisfying and fulfilling for the individual with the illness. Our responsibility is to recognize the symptoms and help them seek the proper care and treatment.

—∾— *Chapter Three* —∾—

Seeking Treatment for Mental Illness

"WHAT DO YOU WANT?"

During a program meeting for members of the Alliance for the Mentally Ill, Dr. Ronald Diamond told a story about a woman he was seeing in a mental institution. When he walked in the room, she was sitting on the floor, rocking back and forth, not making eye contact. He tried to engage her in a conversation, but she wouldn't reply. Finally, out of desperation, Dr. Diamond asked her one question. He said, "What do you want?" And she replied, "I want to go to a restaurant and have a prime rib dinner." This, in Dr. Diamond's words was, "the beginning of a conversation."

If taking a person to a restaurant for a prime rib dinner makes a difference in that person's recovery, then perhaps that's the place to start. If an individual with a mental illness says she wants to get a part-time job, then medical professionals, case workers, and family members can focus their energies on making it possible. Getting a job for a person with schizophrenia or depression may involve a series of steps and a tremendous time commitment. Depending on the severity of the illness and the willingness of the person, the process may have to be carried out in stages, starting with taking medications on a regular basis, getting plenty of sleep, eating balanced meals, and being willing to learn job skills from a job training coach. But in the end, all of these steps lead to something rewarding, something she really wants to do.

According to Dr. Diamond, one of the skills mental health professionals and families need to acquire is the ability to develop a relationship with the person with a mental illness so they find out what motivates the person. Instead of focusing attention on the jobs the person lost, the failed marriages, the fact that the person hears voices or is watching television eight hours a day; Diamond encourages medical professionals and family members to find some method of getting to a place where a conversation begins and a connection is established.

A simple question like "What do you want?" may or may not work in all situations, but it redirects our approach so we look for ways to focus on the motivations, goals, dreams, and aspirations of the person, rather than what is wrong with the individual.

When medical professionals, psychiatrists, family members, and case workers begin to be aware of the goals for treatment, the need for forced hospitalizations or quick fix solutions decreases. The goals for treatment, according to Dr. Diamond, include stability, social control/safety of society, improved function, and recovery—having a life apart from having an illness.

Here are ten significant factors for making decisions related to treatment and decreasing the need for forced hospitalization:

1. Take a long-term view of treatment. Place more emphasis on ongoing care rather than episodic care.

2. Start with the person's own agenda. Ask the person what he or she wants. Knowing what the person wants in the long run provides a focus for treatment.

3. Put treatment into the context of the person's life. Be concrete and realistic. For example, how will the medications help the person with his or her own goals?

4. Make sure that the treatment plan is working—if not, why not?

5. Involve the person as much as possible in decisions about his or her own treatment.

6. Make sure the person with the mental illness, family members, and other persons involved in the overall care know about the treatment plan and options.

7. Be willing to involve friends, family, landlord, clergy, and others, as appropriate, as confidentiality allows, as it fits into the person's own goals and agendas.

8. Be willing to be tenacious when necessary. Start with the person's own agenda. Pay close attention to the relationship with the individual. Take the time to build a relationship. Use crisis as an opportunity to connect.

9. Stay connected to the person even if he or she refuses treatment or parts of treatment.

10. Use forced hospitalization when:
   • No other alternatives are available,
   • Risks of not being hospitalized are too great,
   • Long-term advantages outweigh the long-term disadvantages.[1]

Seeking a Professional Evaluation

Once a family member or friend detects a possible mental illness, it is critical to seek advice from a psychiatrist or physician to set up an evaluation or assessment of the individual. In many cases, this can be done on an outpatient basis. Involuntary treatment or forced hospitalization is not the only alternative for persons suffering from a mental illness. In fact, it may cause damage in the long run. Dr. Diamond suggests a careful look at mental health care options.

In a program meeting of the National Alliance for the Mentally Ill, Dr. Diamond shared some of his insights about forced hospitalization, "The people who have been directly coerced repeat similar phrases. They say that no one listened to them. They say that they felt the forced treatment was unjust.

They say the psychiatrist was not attentive. They say they felt as though they were not being heard." Diamond added that many of his patients remembered the way they were treated unjustly ten or fifteen years after the forced hospitalization.

Dr. Diamond does not deny the fact that there are emergency situations that require a person with mental illness to be hospitalized, perhaps against the person's will. A suicide attempt, for example, often requires immediate hospitalization and treatment. Other situations may not be as clearcut. Diamond illustrated his point with this anecdote, "If I walk out of a building and a brick falls on my head and a friend of mine notices I am behaving differently than I normally do, he may suggest I go the hospital to see if something is wrong with me. Sometimes people do have to undergo surgery against their will, but people don't live in intensive care units," he added, comparing the urgency of treatment for a mental illness to the treatment for a medical emergency.

Forms of Treatment

Finding a good doctor, counselor,
or other medical professional

"The best way to find a good doctor for schizophrenia or any other disease is to ask others in the medical profession whom they would send their own family to if they had a similar problem," suggests Dr. E. Fuller Torrey in his book, *Surviving Schizophrenia*.[2] Another resource is other families who have a family member with an illness. It may be helpful to interview the doctor to find out if he or she is going to be a good match for your relative. Asking the doctor open-ended questions about his or her views on the causes of mental illness, methods of treatment, goals for therapy, and opinion about medications can be beneficial. A good doctor is knowledgeable, compassionate, and an attentive listener.

Depending on the needs of your family member, you may want to consult other medical professionals or counselors. If the doctor you are considering prefers to do routine medication checks without counseling, you may decide to choose a psychologist or counselor for extensive talk therapy. Again, ask the professional therapist if it would be possible to interview him or her, so you have information about the person's background and expertise.

Medication

In a recent survey posted on the National Alliance for the Mentally Ill Web site, a question read: What have you found most helpful in your recovery with mental illness?

Based on the responses, the results were:
- 48 percent medications
- 14 percent therapy
- 20 percent supportive people
- 3 percent alternative medicine
- 8 percent stable housing
- 7 percent employment

The results of this survey correspond to the evidence from medical professionals, case workers, and social workers. **If there is one factor that is the most effective in treating mental illness, it is medication.** However, this doesn't mean that just taking medication alone will bring about full recovery or that one medication will work for all persons with the same illness. Sometimes it takes time to determine the proper medication and dosage. **Treatment that involves a combination of medication, therapy, and a supportive living environment provides the best overall results.**

For persons with affective disorders, such as bipolar illness and depression, medications have a high rate of effectiveness. Lithium carbonate is effective for about 80 percent of the people diagnosed with bipolar illness. However, for the remaining 20 percent of people, this medication is not effective.

According to the National Institute of Mental Health, the success rate for treatment of clinical depression is 80-90 percent, in contrast to the success rate for cardiovascular disease, which is only 45-50 percent. Successful treatment depends on whether the patient finds a medication suited to him or her and works cooperatively with a doctor to receive therapy. Some of the medications commonly prescribed for depression are: Paxil, Prozac (Fluoxetine), Remeron (Mirtazapine), and Zoloft.

Schizophrenia is also treatable. About 80 percent of the people who have schizophrenia respond to medications, but the range of reducing psychotic symptoms vary. For instance, a person who hears voices may notice that the medication reduces the volume of the voices, or makes the voices happen less frequently, or not at all. Other symptoms of schizophrenia such as lack of motivation, verbal responsiveness, or poor self-care may not be affected by taking the more traditional types of antipsychotic medications. However, newer medications such as Clozapine and Risperidone do help these symptoms. Some of the most common medications used to treat schizophrenia are: Clozapine, Zyprexa (Olanzapine), and Risperdal.

One of the difficulties in making decisions about medications is balancing the positive effects of the medications with some of the negative aspects—the side effects. This is especially true of some of the medications for schizophrenia. The side effects may occur before he or she is aware of the therapeutic impact of the medication. For this reason, it is helpful for family members to be informed about the side effects—good and bad—of the medication the person is taking. Family members can give case workers and medical professionals specific information about the patient's progress or lack of progress if they are aware of these effects, any changes in dosage, or refusal to take the medications prescribed. All of the medications listed have some risks and side effects, so it is important for medical professionals to communicate regularly with the individuals who are being treated to find the most effective medication.

COMMUNITY SUPPORT PROGRAMS (CSP)

Community Support Programs provide a wide range of support services for persons with mental illness. Staff, case workers, job coaches, and doctors work together to develop a treatment plan for the individual client. They also provide supportive counseling, ensure regular contact with a case manager, provide frequent medication checks, family therapy, employment and vocational training, social and recreational training, financial support, and transportation to buy groceries or to go to a doctor's appointment.

The PACT (Program of Assertive Community Treatment) program, developed at Mendota Mental Health Institute in Madison, Wisconsin, in 1972, is one of the models for CSPs throughout the country and the world.

TALK THERAPY

Talk therapy is an opportunity for the person with a mental illness or family members to discuss issues related to daily life or interactions. A good therapist provides guidance and direction in dealing with practical matters involving relationships with friends, family, or the mental health system; work-related issues; problem-solving methods; crises; ways to reduce stress; and other matters such as finances or medications. It is helpful if the therapist is able to build a long-term, ongoing relationship in order to provide continuity in treatment. For persons with mood disorders, such as depression, cognitive restructuring may be part of the overall talk therapy. Cognitive restructuring concentrates on helping people evaluate their negative thoughts by reviewing all the information in their life—including the positive and neutral events. Cognitive therapy involves changing thought patterns that contribute to depressive moods.

REDUCING STRESS

Designing strategies to reduce stress can be beneficial for family members and persons with mental illness. This may take the form of simply writing down the things that trigger high levels of stress and presenting the list to a therapist or doctor to discuss. In one therapy session, a therapist asked a person with depression to write down five things she would do if she started to plummet into a depression. These were the five things she wrote down:

1. call a friend
2. pray
3. listen to music
4. do something for someone else
5. write some thank-you notes.

As simple as these activities seem, the comfort of having a brief list to direct the person to do one thing at a time, instead of frantically trying to do either fifty things or nothing at all, seemed to work for her. Every individual has different ways of reducing stress in life.

A man with bipolar illness told me that reducing stress was one of the keys for him in managing his illness. Steven told me he keeps a mental list of things that help him stay relaxed and healthy. The list included getting plenty of rest, paying his bills on time, being social, being aware of changes in relationships, time for exercise, gardening, eating well, and watching sports. Instead of getting anxious if he found himself wide awake at four in the morning (a reminder of the manic phase of his illness, and thus something that could cause a great deal of stress), Steven learned to relieve the anxiety and begin his daily routine as he usually would with coffee, breakfast, and time to read the newspaper. He realized that he might have to catch up on his sleep later in the day, but he allowed himself time to do that. This strategy kept him from fretting or worrying about not getting sleep.

A mother of a young man with schizophrenia found mealtimes stressful. Sometimes when she cooked a special dinner for her son, he would not eat it. But then, two hours later he would ask her for food. Instead of being on constant alert to prepare meals for her son, she decided to stock her refrigerator with healthy snacks, so on the days her son visited he could help himself to the food and eat the meals she prepared when he was hungry. This strategy reduced stress for both the mother and the son.

CREATIVE EXPRESSION

Creative expression provides an outlet for communicating a whole range of emotions. It is a way to order or shape feelings and experiences into a tangible form. Poets, composers, painters, and writers throughout history have discovered new ways to communicate these profound feelings and deepest stirrings in the human mind, heart, and imaginations by giving form to their own personal thoughts and feelings. Often they wrote or sang or painted without ever intending to make their works public.

In her book, *Touched with Fire*, Kay Redfield Jamison sheds light on the mysterious connection between artistic expression and mental illness. What is so striking about Jamison's book is the overwhelming number of artists, who were battling conflicts in their minds, yet found the inner resources to create works of art that affirmed life and hope. Fortunately, these artists had the ability to create in spite of their illness. For if their spirits had been crushed so much that they could not work, the world of music, art, painting, writing, and poetry would be impoverished. What we remember about these artists is the resounding voice and irrepressible spirit to create and be expressive—to paint, to write, to sing, to compose, and to celebrate what is at the heart of being human and being alive. Their works bring meaning to our lives each day. Their expressions resonate with sublime beauty, hope, and connection with the human spirit.

FRIENDSHIP

Persons with mental illness and their families need friendships to sustain them through difficult times. It may seem peculiar to include this topic in a chapter on seeking treatment, because in most cases it is not mentioned as a traditional method for treatment. But I am convinced that friendships have made an enormous difference for me in coping with my own experience with depression and my experience with my brother. Having a mental illness is often accompanied by long hours of isolation and solitude. Sometimes, it is the choice of the person to seek quiet and solitude. Other times, it is not. One true friend can break through the barriers of prejudice with an encouraging word and listening ear.

At the core of treatment of persons with mental illness and the family members involved is the quest to find out who the person is and what the person wants in life. Mental illness often masks the true person. Medications, community support systems, medical professionals, therapy sessions, strategies to reduce stress, creative expression, and friendship all work to get at the heart of who the person is and enable the person to function at the highest level possible.

—∞— Chapter Four —∞—
Finding the Support You Need

Mental illness feeds on isolation. Recovery relies on support.

Nancy Abraham, a parent of a son with schizophrenia, has worked on issues related to mental illness for more than twenty-four years. Her method of learning how to cope with her son's mental illness in the late 1970s has given thousands of family members and individuals a lifeline to education, research, advocacy, and support. She was one of the thirteen parents and family members who started the local chapter of the National Alliance for the Mentally Ill in Madison, Wisconsin, in April 1977. Today, there are more than 210,000 members of the National Alliance for the Mentally Ill, made up of family members, friends, and individuals who seek and provide support, education, and equitable services for persons with mental illnesses.

One of the most important steps in dealing with mental illness started when Nancy decided to talk about her son's illness. "I was one of the first at that time who would stand up in front of a group of people and say, 'I am the parent of an adult child with schizophrenia.' Others didn't feel comfortable saying this aloud," she said. Of course, Nancy did not only *talk* about her son's illness, she started organizing support groups for other parents and family members, started program meetings to educate others, and worked to advocate for the rights of persons with mental illness. And she is still working actively and with enormous determination twenty-four years later.

When I asked Nancy what she thought would be the most important pieces of information I could pass along to others about mental illness, she said, "We need to begin to understand that these illnesses that seem uncommon are very common. And," she added, "serious mental illnesses are disorders of the brain, not something caused by families."

Nancy's suggestions concur with much of the literature written about schizophrenia. In Dr. Fuller Torrey's book, *Surviving Schizophrenia*, he emphasizes the importance of developing a right attitude about the disease.

> Developing the right attitude is the single most important thing an individual or family can do to survive schizophrenia. The right attitude evolves naturally once there is resolution of the twin monsters of schizophrenia—blame and shame. These lie just beneath the surface of many families, impeding the family from moving forward, souring relations between family members, and threatening to explode in a frenzy of fingerpointing, accusations, and recriminations.
>
> People do not cause schizophrenia; they merely blame each other for doing so.[1]

SAFE: DEVELOPING THE RIGHT ATTITUDE

Once blame and shame have been put aside, according to Dr. Torrey, the right attitude toward schizophrenia naturally evolves. There are four elements involved in what he calls the SAFE attitude: sense of humor, acceptance of the illness, family balance, and expectations that are realistic.

Sense of Humor

Although it seems inappropriate to view schizophrenia with a sense of humor, "without humor the family loses its resiliency to handle the inevitable ups and downs inherent in the disease."[2] Having a sense of humor doesn't imply laughing *at* a person with the illness, but laughing *with* them. Dr. Torrey writes about the time he sent his sister with schizophrenia a new suit as a gift. Her reply to the gift was, "the suit looks ghastly on me and I gave it away."[3] Torrey enjoyed the humor of this reply, the sheer honesty and ingenuity of his sister to tell him exactly what she did, instead of following the accepted social graces.

Acceptance of the Illness

Acceptance does not mean the family members give up on the illness, but recognize it as real. Family members need to accept the fact that the person with the illness will have some limitations in his or her abilities. Once a family can accept the illness, there is a great sense of relief and release. "One mother wrote about her sick daughter's reaction when the daughter fully realized her diagnosis and that she had been the 1 in 100 to get the disease: 'Well, I guess if it's percentage-wise,' the daughter said, 'it might as well be me. I have such a terrific family to hold my hand, and because I've been tagged someone else has escaped.'"[4] This type of statement demonstrates a tremendous amount of acceptance and insight.

Family Balance
Developing the right attitude about mental illness also involves balancing the needs of other members in the family. If a family pours all its energies, time, money, and support into one member of the family, other members will most likely suffer. It is important to be able to weigh the conflicting needs of the family with thoughtfulness and care. Parents may need respite if they are the sole caregivers for a person with mental illness. Siblings may need the reassurance and time to know that they are loved and valued. Parents may need to communicate to the person with mental illness that his or her needs do not always come first.

Expectations That Are Realistic
Some parents and family members create unrealistic expectations for their children or siblings, thinking that someday the illness will just go away and the person will become normal again. Some families deal with unfulfilled hopes by having no expectations whatsoever. Dr. Torrey suggests, "Expectations must be realistic . . . and consonant with the capabilities of

the person with schizophrenia. Just as the family of a polio victim should not expect the person's legs to return to complete normality, so too the family of a person with schizophrenia should not expect the person's brain to return to complete normality."[5] Realistic expectations are whatever goals are attainable for the person with the illness. If a person with schizophrenia was skillful playing the piano before he or she became ill, it is likely he or she will continue to play, but with a more limited capacity.

These four elements that Dr. Torrey has identified as useful to develop a right attitude toward schizophrenia also pertain to affective disorders, such as depression and bipolar illness. Again, the causes of these diseases are due to biochemical changes in the brain and the impact of the disease may restrict a person's capabilities.

Community Support

Persons with mental illness crave companionship just as much as all of us, but it is very difficult for them to initiate and participate in at times. Above all, family members, coworkers, neighbors, friends, and church members need to stay connected to these people through the difficult and good times.

Often the families and persons with mental illness are isolated because of stigma. Treating others with affection and compassion is not the cure for mental illness, or the ultimate treatment, but it is a way to build connections with the person and may eventually lead to a path of recovery.

One of the most harmful and debilitating ways to treat persons with mental illness is to spread rumors or ostracize them from the community. Many people with mental illness choose a method of staying in touch with others through creative expression, sports, books, church involvement, or other activities. We do a disservice if we prejudge these individuals or isolate them because they may not fit into society's concept of being sociable. With this in mind, it is critical to be tenacious with phone calls, letters, and invitations to family gatherings and social events to give a strong message of affirmation and support.

Finally, family members need to tap into the wide range of community support programs available for persons with mental illness. Most cities offer a support safety net including medical professionals, case workers, job coaches, housing specialists, and support groups. One of the most successful programs in the country was developed in Madison, Wisconsin, in 1972. The PACT program offers a wide range of assertive outreach, treatment, and rehabilitation for persons with mental illness. The PACT program team includes doctors, psychiatrists, social workers, substance abuse counselors, nurses, and vocational counselors to assist in meeting the needs of their clients. The team of professionals provide services around the clock, seven days a week and 365 days a year. Contact your local National Alliance for the Mentally Ill office to find out what specific community support programs are available in your area or call their HelpLine at 1-800-950-6264 or visit their Web site at www.nami.org.

Financial Concerns

One of the most difficult decisions for family members living with a person with a mental illness is how to pay for hospitalizations, psychiatric visits, medications, and continued medical treatment. The question, "How much will it cost?" becomes such an obstacle that it prevents some individuals and families from seeking any treatment at all. Because of the wide range of federal and state laws pertaining to financial assistance for persons with disabilities, it is important to contact your local Social Security Administration for information on cash benefits. The most common programs available are Social Security Disability Insurance (SSDI) and the Supplemental Security Income Program (SSI).

The National Alliance for the Mentally Ill is one of the most valuable resources for families and persons with mental illness. Information about community support programs, financial assistance, research, questions about medications, and other pertinent information is available. In addition, there is a list of supportive agencies and resources at the end of this book.

—✦— *Chapter Five* —✦—
Living in Hope

How do we *respond* to the fact that one of our family members has been diagnosed with a mental illness? Our response to mental illness is at the core of our own methods of designing tools or strategies to cope with the daily challenges and choices. How do we turn a situation that seems "hope-less" into something that is "hope-filled" or even full of promise?

Hope begins when we face the situation before us and work at it one step at a time. As Anne Lamott writes in her book *Bird by Bird*, "Hope is a revolutionary patience. Hope begins in the dark, the stubborn hope that if you just show up and try to do the right thing, the dawn will come. You wait and watch and work: you don't give up."[1]

Initial responses from parents of children with mental illness ring true for many family members:

"I was shocked."

"I couldn't believe what was happening."

"I felt powerless."

"I saw them look at me as if they were saying, 'What did you do to your kid?'"

"Suddenly my son is sick and I don't know what to do."

In spite of these statements of bewilderment, confusion, and uncertainty, parents and family members usually do know what to do. They ask for help, they take their child to a hospital, or they call a doctor. Rarely do you hear a parent of a child with mental illness say, "I didn't know what was happening with my child, so I just ignored him."

Finding Safe Places

In most cases, the parents can't stand back and passively wait to see what happens. There is an incident or situation that calls for an urgent response, calls for attention, calls for action. Being in a state of uncertainty about a child or family member's health is frightening for anyone, but especially for parents if the person who is ill cannot communicate what's happening. It's similar to parents caring for a newborn child. If the child becomes sick, it is difficult to know what the cause of the illness is and what to do, because the child has no vocabulary other than crying to communicate his pain. Parents of persons with mental illness find comfort and relief when they are able to do something to ensure the safety of their child. One parent put it this way, "One burden had been taken off my shoulders—he was safe." Finding a safe place for the person with the illness is one of the first steps family members can take.

Education

Once the initial shock of discovering the illness is over, family members can begin to educate themselves on the specifics of the mental illness by asking doctors, professionals, and social workers questions or reading literature on the topic, just as they would if their child, spouse, or sibling was hospitalized for a medical emergency. Depending on the severity of the illness and the willingness of the patient, medical professionals may present recommendations to the individual and family members for a wide range of treatments and recovery strategies including: medications, ongoing therapy, handling stressful situations, monitoring moodswings, and finding meaningful work.

"I took a course on schizophrenia," said one parent. "Education about the illness made an enormous difference." Another parent claimed that staying in contact with other parents helped. "I was told to be in contact with people who are healthy and have a common interest," she said.

SHARING EXPERIENCES AND LEARNING FROM OTHERS

Seeking out other parents or family members who have experience dealing with mental illness is another way to move toward a hopeful response. Sharing stories with other family members can generate new insights and perspectives on the daily challenges, whether it is finding out how to plan the holiday gatherings, how to address financial concerns, or how others deal with anger and outbursts.

I'll never forget the Sibling Support Group I attended when my brother was in the initial stages of treatment. I was struck by the laughter in the room. At first it didn't seem appropriate, but I realized that we weren't laughing at the people with the illness. We were laughing at our own feeble attempts to interact and make sense out of the new family dynamics. For me, the laughter was connected to healing and hope. Narratives equip us with examples of family interactions that work and don't work. There is no set formula for families to follow. Each family member has a unique personality and a unique set of experiences developed over many years. But, over time, patterns begin to develop. And recognizing those patterns can bring about more stability and less unpredictability in family interactions.

EMOTIONAL VERSATILITY

One of the most difficult lessons for family members to learn is how to balance love and concern for the person with a healthy dose of detachment. A classic example of this kind of dilemma happens when the person with mental illness becomes outraged about a seemingly insignificant matter in the presence of a family member. For example, a father takes his son to a grocery store and the son doesn't like the way the checkout clerk is looking at him. The son doesn't say anything about the woman until he is in the car and then he unloads all his anger on his father. The son raises his voice and uses expletives. How does the father respond to this? His son's anger could easily set off a chain reaction in the father, even though the father had nothing at all to do with the exchange. But the father chooses to detach himself from the emotional outburst and attends to his own emotional health. As a parent, the father has learned to set limits on the way his son may try to manipulate him. The father has learned to take care of himself and have his own life. One parent said, "I have to live my life as best as I can." Another said, "You have to keep your own sanity."

PERSISTENCE

A foundation of hope is built from a step-by-step approach to make conscious decisions toward mental health and wholeness. Each of us arrives at different stages of enlightenment along the path of our own understanding of mental illness.

To illustrate this, I'd like to share a story from my own family's experience. At the time when my brother was diagnosed with schizophrenia, my father was serving as a senior pastor at a church in southern Wisconsin. Finding out my brother was mentally ill caused a great deal of anguish and grief for both my parents, so much that my father had trouble carrying out his duties as a senior pastor. Members of the church were aware of Dave's illness and recognized the impact it had on my parents. But few members asked about how they could bring comfort or be supportive. They didn't know how to cope with the situation. One trauma led to another. Eventually, my father was asked to leave. After thirty-five years in the ministry, my parents' lives came to standstill. But they didn't give up.

My father was called to interview for a position as pastor at a church in Madison. During the interview process, he told the call committee he had a son with a mental illness; he wanted the members to be aware that he was struggling with a difficult life situation. The call committee hired my father. With four other pastors on staff, the senior pastor invited him to choose a special area of ministry. He chose Outreach Ministry—he wanted to develop a ministry that would extend the hospitality of the church to all members, especially those persons with mental illness and families dealing with mental illness. This became a turning point in his ministry. For the past twenty-three years, my father and mother have been actively involved in educating church members through a program my father developed called *Harnessing the Energies of Love*. It provides practical information for families to prepare for life transforming situations—such as cancer, grief and loss, divorce, alcoholism, and hospitalization.

𝓐 "Hope-Filled" Life

Over the years I have watched my parents create a "hope-filled" life from a seemingly "hope-less" situation. To this day, my father does not bear a grudge against the members of the church who forced him to leave. He has come to realize that they were working within the confines of their own understanding of what mental illness was. They didn't know the causes of mental illness. They didn't know about the different forms of treatment or recovery. They had not been educated about what to do or what to say. They were probably responding out of fear. But experiencing their inability to accept mental illness transformed my parents' perspective; it boosted them into a whole new realm of understanding and acceptance. My parents have lived in hope. They had plenty of reasons to throw up their hands and say, "I give up." They had plenty of excuses to be bitter or resentful or live in despair over the disappointments or hardships. But they didn't choose that way of life.

Because of their experiences as parents of a son with schizophrenia, they have redirected their lives in a way that encourages others to face difficult challenges, to accept responsibilities, to find ways to stay informed, and to learn how to stay connected to people.

FINDING SOLACE AND STRENGTH IN SPIRITUAL RESOURCES

I have also learned from my parents that the deepest reservoir of hope comes from God's steadfast and abundant love. Hope is not something outside of us, something we achieve or grasp in moments of desperation. It is within us, in abundance, as a gift from God. At those times when we feel we are most vulnerable, weak, and tired, God lifts us up and carries us through the experience. Through prayer and constant attention to the ways God works in our lives, we persevere.

One of the major themes in the Bible is God's promise to be with us in all circumstances. It is God's response, a promise of love, acceptance and hope. It gives me great comfort to know that I am not alone in my illness, I am not alone in embracing my brother. God will guide me, other family members will provide support, doctors and counselors will be there in times of crisis, and because of this, I will not give up. These are some of the tools I have been given to keep me moving in the direction of wellness and wholeness.

We may not know exactly what lies ahead when we are living with a family member with mental illness, but we can live in hope as we move through the stages of acceptance. We ask for help. We provide a safe environment for ourselves and the person who is ill. We educate ourselves about the illness and the treatment options. We seek support from other family members and listen to their stories. We develop emotional versatility, so we are not swept away by the emotions of the person who is ill. And we find solace in spiritual resources, knowing God is present and active in our lives. Our trust in God sustains us through the times of uncertainty. As Paul writes in the book of Romans,

> We continue to shout our praise even when we're hemmed in with troubles, because we know how trouble can develop passionate patience in us, and how that patience in turn forges the tempered steel

of virtue, keeping us alert for whatever God will do next. In alert expectancy such as this, we're never left feeling shortchanged. Quite the contrary—we can't round up enough containers to hold everything God generously pours into our lives through the Holy Spirit! (Romans 5:2-5)[2]

In closing, I offer this prayer:

Dear Lord,
You have promised to be present in our lives in all circumstances. You have given us the gift of life and love, compassion and acceptance, forgiveness and hope. Teach us to love all persons, especially those who are struggling with mental and emotional illnesses. Give courage and strength to family members so they find relief in the daily struggles in their lives. Show us how to reassure them and give them hope. Give us the tools to reach out to them with words of encouragement and healing. Protect them from injustice and prejudice. Make us aware of ways we can build bridges of understanding through education, research, support, and advocacy, so all persons with mental illness will have satisfying and fulfilling lives. In Jesus Christ's name, Amen.

—∞— *Notes* —∞—

CHAPTER 2

1. National Health Advisory Council. "Health Care Reform for Americans with Severe Mental Illnesses." American Journal of Psychiatry 150:10 (1993), 1450-1452.
2. *The AMI—Wisconsin Family and Consumer Resource Guide,* edited by Jennifer Ondrejka, Third Edition, 1996, 3.
3. *Ibid.,* 3-4.
4. *Ibid.,* 4.
5. *Ibid.,* 6.
6. National Alliance for the Mentally Ill. "Understanding Major Depression: What You Need to Know about This Medical Illness." Pamphlet, 6.
7. *Ibid.,* 7
8. Mental Health Association in Milwaukee County. "Bipolar Disorder." Pamphlet, 2.

CHAPTER 3

1. "A closer look at involuntary treatment."Alliance for the Mentally Ill Newsletter of Dane County, *The Pioneer,* V. 22, No. 4, (April 2001),1.
2. Dr. E. Fuller Torrey, *Surviving Schizophrenia: A Manual for Families, Consumers, and Providers* (Third Edition), New York: Harper Collins, 1995, 176.

CHAPTER 4

1. Dr. E. Fuller Torrey, *Surviving Schizophrenia: A Manual for Families, Consumers, and Providers* (Third Edition), New York: Harper Collins, 1995, 280.
2. Ibid., 284.
3. Ibid., 284.
4. Ibid., 285
5. Ibid., 285.

CHAPTER 5

1. Anne Lamott, introduction to *Bird by Bird: Some Instructions on Writing and Life.* (New York: Doubleday, 1994), p. Introduction, xxiii.
2. Scripture quotations from *The Message.* Copyright © by Eugene H. Peterson 1993, 1994, 1995. Used by permission of NavPress Publishing Group.

—∞— *Resources* —∞—

National Alliance for the Mentally Ill
200 North Glebe Road
Suite 1015
Arlington, VA 22203-3754.
Telephone: (703) 524-7600 or toll free at 1-800-950-NAMI
Web site: www.nami.org

National Institute of Mental Health
5600 Fishers Lane
Room 15C-05
Rockville, MD 20857
(301) 443-4513
Web site: www.nimh.nih.gov

National Depressive and Manic Depressive Association
Merchandise Mart
Box 3395
Chicago, IL 60654
(312) 939-2442
Web site: www.ndmda.org

American Psychiatric Association
1400 K Street, N.W.
Suite 1101
Washington, D.C. 20005
(202) 682-6000
Web site: www.psych.org

National Mental Health Association
1021 Prince Street
Alexandria, VA 23314-2971
(703) 684-7722
Web site: www.nmha.org

National Empowerment Center, Inc.
599 Canal Street
Lawrence, MA 01840
(978) 685-1518
Web site: www.power2u.org

The Centre for Mental Health Solutions
6950 France Avenue South
Suite 18
Minneapolis, MN 55435
952-922-6916
Web site address: www.tcfmhs.org

—∞— *Bibliography* —∞—

JOURNALS AND PAMPHLETS

"A closer look at involuntary treatment." Alliance for the
    Mentally Ill Newsletter of Dane County, *The Pioneer* 22,
    no. 4, (April 2001).

"Bipolar Disorder," Mental Health Association in Milwaukee
     County Pamphlet.
"Health Care Reform for American with Severe Mental Ill-
     nesses." *American Journal of Psychiatry* 150 no. 10
     (1993) National Health Advisory Council, 1450-1452.
"Understanding Major Depression: What You Need to Know
     about This Medical Illness." National Alliance for the
     Mentally Ill Pamphlet.

BOOKS

Jamison, Kay Redfield. *Touched with Fire: Manic-Depressive
     Illness and the Artistic Temperament.* New York: Free
     Press, 1993.

Lamott, Anne. *Bird by Bird: Some Instructions on Writing and
     Life.* New York: Doubleday, 1994.

Ondrejka, Jennifer. *The Alliance for the Mentally Ill
     Wisconsin Family and Consumer Resource Guide.*
     3rd ed., 1996.

Peterson, Eugene. *The Message: New Testament with Psalms
     and Proverbs.* Colorado Springs, Colo.: Navpress, 1993.

Torrey, Dr. E. Fuller. *Surviving Schizophrenia: A Manual for
     Families, Consumers, and Providers.* 3rd ed. New York:
     Harper Collins, 1995.

Woolis, Rebecca, M.F.C.C. *When Someone You Love Has a
     Mental Illness: A Handbook for Family, Friends, and
     Caregivers.* New York: Penguin Putnam, 1992.

—ᴡ— *Acknowledgments* —ᴡ—

Thanks to Ron Klug, my editor. Thanks to my parents, Mae and Willard Lund, for their encouragement and determination to face all circumstances in life with perseverance, prayer, and hope. Thanks to my family and friends for their understanding, courage, and buoyant spirit. Thanks to my son, Joe Swiggum, for his love and support. Thanks to Pastor Timothy Fuzzey for inspiring me and encouraging me to share my experience about mental illness with others. Thanks to all the persons I interviewed as preparation for this book. I am grateful for all your stories and contributions.

Other Resources from Augsburg

Through the Wilderness of Alzheimer's
by Robert and Anne Simpson
160 pages, ISBN 0-8066-3891-5

In telling the story of their journey into
Alzheimer's, the Simpsons offer accu-
rate, firsthand information and help for
caregivers and patients.

Psalms for Healing by Gretchen Person
170 pages, ISBN 0-8066-4161-4

A thoughtful collection of psalms and
prayers for those who seek healing.

Prayers for Help and Healing
by William Barclay
128 pages, ISBN 0-8066-2784-0

For people in crisis and their caregivers,
William Barclay has written these simple,
practical, and comforting prayers.

Available wherever books are sold.
To order these books directly, contact:
1-800-328-4648 • www.augsburgfortress.org
Augsburg Fortress, Publishers
P.O. Box 1209, Minneapolis, MN 55440-1209

CPSIA information can be obtained at www.ICGtesting.com
Printed in the USA
LVOW010957200113

316433LV00001B/117/P

3 4711 00217 2213